LIVING WITH
ANXIETY DISORDERS

LIVING WITH ANXIETY DISORDERS

by Carol Hand

Content Consultant
Jeremy K. Fox, PhD, Department of Psychology,
Montclair State University

LIVING WITH HEALTH CHALLENGES

CREDITS

Published by ABDO Publishing Company, PO Box 398166, Minneapolis, MN 55439. Copyright © 2014 by Abdo Consulting Group, Inc. International copyrights reserved in all countries. No part of this book may be reproduced in any form without written permission from the publisher. The Essential Library™ is a trademark and logo of ABDO Publishing Company.

Printed in the United States of America,
North Mankato, Minnesota
092013
012014

Editor: Melissa York
Series Designer: Becky Daum

Photo credits: Andrey Shadrin/Shutterstock, cover, 3; Comstock/Thinkstock, 8, 86; iStockphoto/Thinkstock, 11, 18, 26, 28, 35, 38, 48, 55, 60, 65, 68, 71, 76, 95; Fuse/Thinkstock, 14, 58, 78; Monkey Business/Thinkstock, 16; Jupiterimages/Thinkstock, 32; FogStock/Thinkstock, 46; VStock/Thinkstock, 52; Stockbyte/Thinkstock, 80; Creatas Images/Thinkstock, 88

Library of Congress Control Number: 2013945891

Cataloging-in-Publication Data

Hand, Carol.
 Living with anxiety disorders / Hand, Carol.
  p. cm. -- (Living with health challenges)
Includes bibliographical references and index.
ISBN 978-1-62403-241-7
1. Anxiety--Juvenile literature.   2. Anxiety disorders--Juvenile literature.
I. Title.
616.85--dc23

2013945891

CONTENTS

EXPERT ADVICE

I am a licensed clinical psychologist specializing in cognitive behavioral therapy for children and teenagers with anxiety disorders. From my experience, teenagers are particularly likely to encounter a wide array of challenges and stressors that can trigger anxiety. As school becomes more demanding, teens often feel pressure to achieve, which can lead to anxiety surrounding tests and grades. Peer relationships also become more significant during the teenage years. Common worries can range from where to sit at the lunch table to finding a date for the dance.

At the same time, compared to children, teens are less reliant on their parents for help with managing anxiety. That is why it is so important for youth with anxiety disorders to seek support from qualified mental health professionals as early as possible before their anxieties become excessive and impairing. My key pieces of advice for you are:

Be aware. Know when your anxiety starts becoming a problem. If you leave class because your heart starts racing before a test, you are likely experiencing more excessive and impairing anxiety than if you just have a few butterflies that disappear when tests begin.

Face your fears. Breaking out of avoidance patterns is almost always a critical step in overcoming anxiety disorders. Make a list of situations you are currently avoiding. Order them from least anxiety provoking to most anxiety provoking. Then start by approaching the situations on the bottom of the list and work your way up as you complete them successfully. Doing this on your own may sound like a piece of cake, but it is just as important you find people to help you.

Get support. It can be valuable to work with a mental health professional who can serve as both a guide and a cheerleader along the road to mastering your anxiety. Plus, many individuals experience considerable relief after simply talking with someone about their anxiety. This book can get you started, but it is not a replacement for professional help.

Remember, your anxiety is something that can be managed. Doing so will give you confidence to meet new challenges and embrace important opportunities.

—*Jeremy K. Fox, PhD, Department of Psychology, Montclair State University*

1

WHAT IS AN ANXIETY DISORDER?

Emma was arguing with her mother again. They were making her sophomore class schedule, and her mother was already worried about her future. She wanted Emma to sign up for some extracurricular activities to help her get into a good college.

If you have undiagnosed anxiety disorder, feeling pressure from family members to do activities that make you feel uncomfortable can lead to arguments.

"You have a great singing voice," her mother said. "You should be in choir. And you know so much—you'd be great in Academic Club."

"But I don't want to!" Emma begged. "You know I'm shy. Classes are hard enough. I don't need the extra stress."

Choir might not be so bad, she thought—at least she wouldn't be singing alone—but she would still have to perform in front of everyone. And Academic Club! She cringed at the very thought of having a microphone in front of her and being put on the spot to answer questions. Her mother was right; she would probably know most of the answers. But there was no way she could give an answer in public like that. She couldn't even answer questions in class without blushing and stammering.

Finally, to keep her mother from bugging her, Emma agreed to join choir. Maybe it won't be so bad, she thought. Rehearsals might be okay, and maybe she could plead illness when there was a concert. She didn't say this out loud, of course, but her mother sensed her reluctance and gave her a skeptical look.

Emma sighed. As usual, she wasn't looking forward to school, and it would be even worse now. She knew her anxiety was making her life miserable and that her mother only wanted to help, but she had no idea what to do about it.

ANXIETY DISORDERS

Emma suffers from anxiety. Her worry is out of proportion to the seriousness of the situation, and she can't control it. Anxiety is the worry, nervousness, or dread you feel when you think about some future event. In other words, you're worrying about something that hasn't happened yet and may not ever happen. Fear is a response to a more immediate danger, which may or may not be real.

Anxiety in moderation is perfectly normal—in fact, it's essential to life. Anxiety and fear stimulate the same centers in the brain and cause the same set of reactions— the fight-or-flight response. It is your body's way of

FIGHT-OR-FLIGHT RESPONSE

When you perceive a threat, the brain's hypothalamus region triggers the release of the hormone epinephrine, also called adrenaline. Adrenaline raises blood pressure, heart rate, and breathing rate; increases blood glucose to provide energy; and rushes more blood to the muscles. These changes prepare you for a quick response. Your face gets hot, you tense up, and you tremble or feel jittery. You might have butterflies in your stomach. Under normal conditions, adrenaline quickly dissipates and you feel fine again. But when you have an anxiety disorder, the fight-or-flight symptoms continue.

*A near miss with a car can set off
your fight-or-flight response.*

preparing you to respond quickly to threats. In
case of a physical threat—a dog growls and
bares its teeth, or a car comes roaring down
the street toward you—fear takes over and your
body responds instantly. A rush of adrenaline
causes you to run from the danger before the
thinking centers of your brain can react. If you
had to stop and think about the threat, you might
not react quickly enough. The fight-or-flight
response makes you alert, focused, and able
to react instantly to danger. In extreme cases,
anxiety can save your life. When the threat is
passed, the physical symptoms quickly abate.

Sometimes the threat is further in the future
and is not physical. You might be anxious about

passing your math test or worry about how you'll perform in the upcoming football game. In these cases, anxiety is perfectly normal and can help you do your best. But sometimes your body overreacts and becomes too anxious. The physical symptoms of the fight-or-flight response are too strong and continue for too long. When you are extremely anxious, your mind works overtime, coming up with worst-case scenarios. For example, you worry you will blow the football game and everyone will hate you. Even if you know, deep down, that you are overreacting, you can't help yourself. Negative thoughts can lead to physical symptoms of stress, such as rapid breathing, rapid heartbeat, and sweating.

"NORMAL" ANXIETY VS. ANXIETY DISORDERS

How can you distinguish between "normal" anxiety and a true anxiety disorder? According to Doctors Michael A. Tompkins and Katherine Martinez, it helps to consider the "four Ds of anxiety."

1. "Is your anxiety *disproportionate* to the situation?" Do you worry a lot about things other teens only worry about slightly?

2. "Is your anxiety *disrupting* or interfering with your life?" Does it keep you from doing things you really want to do or make you avoid situations that other teens enjoy?

3. "Is your anxiety *distressing* to you?" Do you do certain things because you feel you have to, but feel extremely uncomfortable while doing them?

4. "What is the *duration* of your anxiety?" Have you been anxious for months about something that is not a problem for most people?[1]

Excessive anxiety might even lead you to extreme actions, such as quitting the football team.

Anxiety becomes a disorder when it is excessive—when your reactions are too intense or long lasting or when they interfere with your life. You might feel unprotected and fear every little thing. You might have feelings of doom or just feel overwhelmed by life. These feelings affect your health, your ability to concentrate, and your interactions with others. In short, they affect your whole life.

GENERAL SYMPTOMS OF ANXIETY

Anxiety disorders vary, and different people are afraid of different things. Not everyone has the same symptoms with the same intensity. In general, anxiety is an emotion, generally described as feeling overwhelmed or edgy, or feeling dread, nervousness, distress, panic, or worry. But some general symptoms are characteristic of anxiety. These are usually classified into physical, behavioral, and cognitive symptoms.

Physical Symptoms

Physical symptoms of anxiety are the same ones seen in the fight-or-flight response. They include feelings of restlessness, shortness of breath, choking, sweaty palms, racing heart,

People with anxiety sometimes try to avoid social situations such as parties.

chest pain, muscle tension, trembling, nausea, diarrhea, hot flashes, cold chills, dizziness, faintness, butterflies in the stomach, numbness, tingling, an exaggerated startle response, and difficulty sleeping.

Behavioral Symptoms

The primary behavioral symptoms, or actions associated with anxiety, include avoiding anxiety-producing places or activities or trying to escape from anxiety-producing situations that you are already in, such as leaving a crowded area. Some avoidance behaviors are overt, such as refusing to go to a party. Others are subtler, such as going to the party, but constantly checking your phone to avoid talking to people. Other people may perform risky or self-destructive behaviors such as drinking or taking drugs to cope with anxiety.

Cognitive Symptoms

Cognitive symptoms are thoughts associated with anxiety. The most characteristic cognitive symptom involves the way an anxious person interprets situations. If you are anxious, you tend to overestimate the threat of a situation and underestimate your own ability to deal with it. You might be easily humiliated or feel you're losing control. In the mind of the anxious person, the slightest difficulty becomes a catastrophe. Other cognitive symptoms include inability to concentrate and memory problems.

These three types of anxiety symptoms may interact with each other and further increase anxiety levels. For example, if you feel physical anxiety symptoms in certain situations, you may choose to avoid those situations. The avoidance of the situations, in turn, prevents you from confronting your anxiety and may ultimately cause more anxiety.

Of course, you cannot diagnose an anxiety disorder by yourself or by reading a book, but if you react to situations with excessive fear,

Anxiety can make it difficult for people to enjoy life.

worry, or dread, or if your anxiety is interfering with your life, it's time to get help. Children, teens, and adults may have anxiety disorders. Anxiety can happen all at once or occur gradually. However it began and whatever you're afraid of, anxiety is not something to be ashamed of. It's just a problem you need to solve, and solving problems is always easier with help. The good news is there are treatments that can help. Talk to a parent, teacher, or counselor about your fears. Together, you can decide how to deal with your anxiety.

ASK YOURSELF THIS

- *Do you have any symptoms of an anxiety disorder? What are they?*

- *Are your symptoms preventing you from doing things you really want to do?*

- *Can you pinpoint the cause of your anxiety, or do you feel afraid at many times or in various situations?*

- *Have you considered ways to decrease your anxiety?*

- *Have you talked to anyone about how you feel or asked for help?*

CHANGES IN DEFINITION OF ANXIETY DISORDERS

Anxiety disorders and other mental disorders are defined and their symptoms listed in a book published by the American Psychiatric Association (APA), *Diagnostic and Statistical Manual of Mental Disorders*. The fifth and newest edition of this manual was released in May 2013. Nicknamed the *DSM-5*, the text incorporates several changes based on the latest research and updates the descriptions psychiatrists and psychologists use to classify these conditions.

2

TYPES OF ANXIETY DISORDERS

Nick was with his friends Andre and Juan. They were hanging out on the bridge in the park, watching water roar through the storm drain. Andre and Juan were laughing about how funny Coach looked when he accidentally dropped the big bottle of water

Sometimes feelings of anxiety or panic are triggered by specific situations, such as standing on a bridge.

he was trying to put on the water cooler. It had been funny—nearly everything was drenched: the floor, Coach, and half of the team.

Maybe it was all the talk of water, or listening to the roaring beneath him, but Nick suddenly felt terrified. He began gasping for breath, and he could feel his heart pounding. He grasped the railing to keep from falling, but he was trembling all over. His friends stopped talking and looked at him in alarm. "Hey, man, what's the matter?" Andre asked. "You look like you've seen a ghost."

Nick couldn't reply. He felt as though he was going to die, and he knew his friends could see the fear in his eyes. He was thoroughly embarrassed, but he couldn't stop the feelings. They led him to a bench and he sat down. Finally, he calmed down and stopped shaking, but he felt like he'd just run a marathon.

Embarrassed or not, he owed his friends an explanation. He explained about his panic attacks. The attacks had started six months ago after a car accident. The car had almost gone off a bridge and he still remembered the roaring water. "This is the first time it's ever happened in front of friends, though," he said. "I'm really sorry, guys."

His friends were sympathetic. They promised to watch him for signs of a panic attack—and to keep him away from roaring water!

Panic attacks, such as the ones Nick has, or panic disorder, in which panic attacks occur "out of the blue," with no obvious trigger, are two of several types of anxiety disorders. Psychologists sometimes tend to place anxiety disorders in neat little boxes, with each type having a specific list of symptoms. Real life is not that simple. No two people have exactly the same set of symptoms. While one form of anxiety usually predominates, the same person might suffer from fears that fit into several categories, and psychologists know this. Doctors treat each fear or anxiety separately. Anxiety disorders are classified into several major types.

GENERALIZED ANXIETY DISORDER

Teens with generalized anxiety disorder (GAD) might worry excessively about nearly anything. GAD usually starts around age 12. A diagnosis is made if the teen has been worrying excessively for six months or more. Approximately two-thirds of teens with GAD are girls.[1] GAD sufferers worry about the same things other teens worry about (such as friends, classmates, school, health, and performance), but their worries are constant and more intense.

Worries about school and sports are most common, but some youth with GAD worry more intensely about "big" things, such as war, personal harm, or disasters.

Teens with GAD are fidgety, restless, and irritable. They have trouble concentrating and sleeping and may have muscle pains, stomach pains, or headaches. They seek constant reassurance, procrastinate, and might try to avoid school and activities. They tend to be perfectionists and have trouble being flexible when plans change.

TEST ANXIETY

So many teens become stressed before exams that this type of anxiety has a name: test anxiety. This is a type of performance anxiety, and worriers and perfectionists tend to have the most trouble with it. You may be well prepared and know the material, yet when the pressure's on, your mind goes blank and you sweat, shake, and feel like throwing up. You dwell on all the bad things that might happen if you do poorly. To minimize test anxiety, prepare for the test, get plenty of sleep, and monitor your thoughts. Just as negative thinking can make you do worse on the test, positive thinking can improve your score.

SEPARATION ANXIETY DISORDER

Separation anxiety—fear of being separated from parents or other caregivers—is common among young children. If it persists after approximately age five and interferes with a child's life, the fear becomes separation anxiety disorder. It can prevent the child or teen from developing normal friendships and joining activities and might affect school attendance and performance. Teens might suffer separation anxiety when changing schools, going through their parents' divorce or the death of a loved one, or going to sleepovers or on school trips.

People with separation anxiety disorder may worry something bad will happen if they separate from a loved one. Before leaving for a scheduled trip or activity, or even school, they might develop physical symptoms of anxiety, such as a stomachache, dizziness, or rapid heartbeat or breathing.

SOCIAL ANXIETY DISORDER

Social anxiety disorder is a fear of social or performance situations in which you are being evaluated, or feel that you are. You may feel self-conscious and fear you will do something embarrassing. Social situations as simple as talking to friends, meeting new people, going to parties, dating, or talking on the phone might trigger social anxiety disorder. Performance-based triggers include participating in class, public speaking, playing on a sports team, acting in a play, or giving a music recital. Some people with social anxiety disorder have one specific fear—for example, public speaking—while others feel anxiety in many social situations. Social anxiety disorder is not the same as being shy, it doesn't mean you're socially inept, and it isn't a "normal" case of nervousness. It's a disorder that causes you to avoid people and activities.

OCD AND PTSD

Until the May 2013 release of the fifth edition of the American Psychiatric Association's *Diagnostic and Statistical Manual of Mental Disorders*, two additional disorders were classified with anxiety disorders. A person with obsessive-compulsive disorder (OCD) constantly performs specific compulsions, such as checking the door locks exactly three times before being able to sleep. These actions are often used to calm disturbing or inappropriate thoughts or obsessions. Common obsessions include fear of germs, getting sick, harming oneself or others, or maintaining exactness and symmetry (for example, arranging items by color or size). Compulsions include excessive hand washing, counting or touching items a certain number of times, or constant mental repetition of a word or number.

Post-traumatic stress disorder (PTSD) can occur in anyone who has suffered a severe trauma and felt extreme fear, horror, or helplessness. People with PTSD may reexperience the traumatic event through recurring memories, flashbacks, or nightmares. They may feel unwilling to remember the event or be around people who or places that trigger memories of it. They may feel emotional numbness, resulting in detaching from people, not enjoying activities, and becoming unable to express emotions. They may have trouble sleeping and concentrating and may be constantly vigilant, irritable, and angry.

SCHOOL REFUSAL AND SELECTIVE MUTISM

School refusal is a disorder in which a child or teen refuses to go to school or has difficulty remaining in school. It occurs most often from ages five to six or ten to 11, after moving, or when entering middle school or high school. It is accompanied by physical symptoms such as headaches, stomachaches, nausea, or diarrhea. Symptoms often appear before school but disappear if the child or teen is allowed to stay home. Another disorder is selective mutism. These teens refuse to talk in specific social situations such as school. They are capable of speaking and do speak at home, but they stop speaking in anxiety-producing situations.

Blushing, trembling, sweaty hands, and freezing up when required to "perform," even if it's only talking to someone, are clues you might have social anxiety disorder. A racing heart, tense muscles, and a stomachache are other giveaways.

PANIC DISORDER

A panic attack is a sudden, spontaneous wave of intense fear and impending doom. It triggers intense physical reactions, including rapid heart rate, sweating, trembling, shortness of breath, and hyperventilation. You may faint or feel as though you're having a heart attack or going crazy. Some people have only one or two panic attacks in a lifetime, but if your attacks are repeated and unexpected, you could have panic disorder.

Isolated panic attacks usually begin around puberty, and full-blown panic disorder appears by late adolescence or early adulthood. Because they are unexpected, each panic attack triggers fear of the next. You avoid places or situations where a panic attack might occur: places you fear, such as tunnels or elevators, or places where an attack occurred before, such as school.

SPECIFIC PHOBIAS

The final category of anxiety disorders consists of specific phobias, which affect more than 10 percent of people and often begin in adolescence.[2] A phobia is an intense, unreasonable fear of a specific object or situation. Specific phobias interfere with your ability to live your life and can even trigger panic attacks. Suppose you have a dog phobia. You become anxious

AGORAPHOBIA

Agoraphobia is a "fear of being in places or situations from which escape might be difficult or in which help might not be available in the event of a panic attack."[3] In the *DSM-5*, agoraphobia is considered a separate disorder. People with agoraphobia avoid being in public or crowded places, such as elevators, shopping malls, sporting events, or airplanes. In these situations, they feel trapped and helpless, and they may suffer symptoms of a panic attack. In extreme situations, people become afraid to leave their own homes.

Fear of heights is one of the most common phobias.

whenever you encounter a dog. You know the fear is irrational and most dogs present no real danger, but you can't control the fear. So, you avoid situations in which you might encounter a dog. Since there are dogs all over your neighborhood, this can seriously limit your activities!

Triggers for an anxiety disorder vary greatly. You might fit into several of these categories. But, regardless of the trigger, you feel great distress, you try to avoid your anxiety trigger or triggers, and you know anxiety is controlling your life. How did you get this way, and what can you do about it?

TYPES OF SPECIFIC PHOBIAS

Phobia triggers fall into five major categories:

- **Animals (dogs, snakes, spiders)**
- **Natural environment (heights, water, storms)**
- **Injury or pain (injections, blood, dentist)**
- **Situational (airplanes, enclosed spaces)**
- **Other (loud noises, choking)**

ASK YOURSELF THIS

- *Do you have symptoms of one or more categories of anxiety disorder? If so, which categories?*

- *What are your symptoms? Which symptoms bother you the most?*

- *Can you identify a trigger for your anxiety or an event that originally caused it?*

- *What are you currently doing to try to deal with your anxiety?*

- *Have you discussed your anxiety with a parent or counselor?*

WHY AM I LIKE THIS?

Aaliyah was recently diagnosed with generalized anxiety disorder, or GAD. She was glad to have a name for her feelings and to know someone would take them seriously. But she also felt embarrassed. After all, who wants to have a mental disorder? And where did it come from?

At her mother's urging, Aaliyah shared her diagnosis with her best friend, Jasmine. Jasmine had always known Aaliyah was timid and afraid of many things, and she asked how she could help. She, too, was curious about why Aaliyah had GAD. They decided to do some research on causes of GAD. "Maybe it's genetic," Jasmine said. "Are other people in your family like you?" Aaliyah considered this. "Well, yes, I guess we are all kind of nervous, especially my mom and aunt. They worry a lot, especially about us kids, whether we're going to get hurt, not do well in school—you name it."

Jasmine read from a pamphlet. "That's probably not all genetics," she said. "Some is probably parenting and role models. You pick up on their anxiety and you get anxious, too."

"Yeah, that's probably true," Aaliyah agreed, "but I'm even more scared and worried than they are. That's why Mom finally got me tested. I was so worried, I couldn't study, and my grades went down. I can't even watch the news. If I hear about a murder or robbery, I can't sleep because I'm afraid the same thing will happen to us."

Jasmine grinned at her. "Yeah, you're a mess, all right. But don't worry—you've got me to keep you on the right track!" Aaliyah knew it wouldn't be easy, but she was thankful to have a good friend like Jasmine.

GENES, PREDISPOSITION, AND TEMPERAMENT

Risk factors for developing anxiety disorders are complex and not completely understood. As Aaliyah and Jasmine discovered, anxiety disorders seem to result from a combination of genetic and environmental factors. Genes affect your personality and the functioning of your brain and hormones. Environmental factors include the type of parenting you receive and your specific life events. Anxiety disorders develop when these genetic and environmental factors interact.

Some people are born with a predisposition to anxiety. That is, your genes might make you more susceptible to anxiety. You may be more likely to have hormone

FACTS ABOUT ANXIETY DISORDERS

- Approximately one in 20 teens has anxiety disorders.[1]
- People between ages 15 and 24 have the most anxiety disorders.[2]
- Girls are more prone to anxiety disorders than boys.[3]
- Approximately half of people diagnosed with depression also have an anxiety disorder.[4]

imbalances, and you might have a parent or sibling with anxiety. Genes control brain and body chemistry, which in turn control behavioral factors such as temperament. Chemicals also control anxiety. The same genes seem to control all types of anxiety and possibly depression as well. A gene called *5-HTT* regulates the amount of the chemical serotonin released by the brain. A *5-HTT* variation that causes low serotonin levels is found in people prone to GAD, panic attacks, and obsessive-compulsive disorder (OCD). Having the variation gives people a predisposition for anxiety disorders. But having a predisposition does not necessarily mean you will have an anxiety disorder. Often, people will have no symptoms unless they suffer extreme stress or trauma.

TODAY'S ANXIOUS TEENS

Today's teens are more anxious than their parents were as teens, and more teens today manage their anxiety with prescription medications. Sometimes, anxiety spreads to teens from parents who work too hard and worry about nearly everything. Teens with divorced parents have added stress. At school, many feel pressure to compete and succeed so they can be accepted into a good college. In a recent British study, girls were two times more likely than boys to describe themselves as anxious. Teens worry about popularity, appearance, careers, pressure to have sex, and living up to the expectations of the glamorous celebrity culture popularized on television. Teens from economically disadvantaged backgrounds tend to be more anxious than teens from more advantaged backgrounds.

Both genetics and how your parents raise you can affect your risk of developing an anxiety disorder.

Your inherited temperament can also affect your likelihood of developing an anxiety disorder. Psychologists classify children along a spectrum from "shy, timid, and inhibited" to "outgoing, bold, and uninhibited."[5] More inhibited children tend to respond to unfamiliar situations by avoidance or distress and have a higher risk of developing anxiety disorders in adolescence or adulthood.

PARENTING AND MODELING

The type of parenting and role models a child grows up with also affect development of anxiety disorders. Some parents are overprotective. They protect their children from even normal childhood activities such as going down a playground slide. Children, particularly those with inhibited temperaments, quickly learn to become fearful of trying new things. It is difficult to determine cause and effect in these situations. That is, does the child become anxious because of overprotection, or does the parent protect the child because the child is already anxious and fearful? Most researchers think both are true.

Children also learn by observing. Role models—including parents—affect the amount of fear and anxiety children develop. If a child watches his or her mother shriek in the presence of a snake, the child will probably learn to fear snakes, too. Likewise, if a child sees playmates or other adults trying

COMORBIDITY

Approximately 40 to 60 percent of anxious children suffer from comorbidity; that is, they have more than one mental disorder.[6] The highest level of comorbidity is between anxiety and depression. A child with an anxiety disorder is 8.2 times more likely to suffer from depression than a nonanxious child.[7] Those who suffer from an anxiety disorder as children are more likely to suffer from the same disorder in adolescence and early adulthood. However, some anxiety disorders disappear as children grow up, and some people first develop anxiety as adults.

new things, the child will be more willing to try them. Verbal cues can also affect anxiety. If a parent frequently warns a child about germs, the child is more likely to fear germs.

ENVIRONMENT AND LIFE EVENTS

Frightening or traumatic life events can trigger or increase anxiety, especially in anxious or inhibited children. Specific environmental events may lead to different types of anxiety disorders. For example, a frightening event in a park when you were small might make you avoid that park or even trigger a panic attack. An embarrassing performance in sports or music might trigger social anxiety that makes it difficult for you to perform thereafter.

Stressful life situations can trigger anxiety, particularly in timid teens with predispositions toward anxiety. Teens who had separation anxiety as small children might develop generalized anxiety disorder. Academic pressures or the need to fit in can overwhelm others. Changing schools or serious family crises such as divorce, death, or homelessness can trigger social anxiety. Many teens feel unsafe at school and elsewhere due to bullies, drug or gang activity, or physical or sexual abuse. Some medical conditions, such as asthma, drug abuse, or alcohol withdrawal, can also cause anxiety.

The causes and triggers of anxiety are complex and everyone experiences the condition differently.

Risk factors for developing anxiety disorders interact in ways that are unique to each individual. All result from some combination of genetics, hormonal imbalances, stressful life experiences, personality, and even physical illness. Their interactions may result in anxiety disorders in some teens, while others may show little effect. In any case, if you have an anxiety disorder, don't blame yourself! This is a medical condition resulting from a complex set of conditions. Once you begin to understand the factors involved in anxiety, you can use this information to overcome your anxiety.

THE ADOLESCENT BRAIN

Anxiety in teens is complicated because the teenage brain is still growing and changing. You will be in your early 20s before your brain is completely developed. In teens, both the intensity of emotional responses and the ability to learn are the highest they will ever be. However, the parts of the brain responsible for adult behavior such as controlling impulses and planning ahead develop late in adolescence. So, while you may have very strong emotional reactions, you may still have difficulty controlling your behavior.

Control of sleeping patterns also changes during adolescence, which may be one reason many teens like to stay up late. But sleep deprivation leads to fatigue, inattention, irritability, and depression, which are often present in anxious teens. Sleep deprivation also increases impulsive behavior. As the brain matures, it helps the teen transition to independence. But many types of anxiety disorders also begin during this time. Research is continuing to determine whether these two things are connected.

ASK YOURSELF THIS

- *Do you think you have a predisposition for anxiety? Why do you think this?*

- *Do you have medical issues, such as hormone imbalances, that might affect your anxiety level?*

- *Do you feel your parents are overprotective? If so, what are some examples?*

- *How do you think you would respond if your parents pushed you more to try new things or interact with new people? Would this make you more or less anxious?*

- *Did you experience any extremely frightening or traumatic events in your childhood?*

CONSEQUENCES OF ANXIETY DISORDERS

When Ethan finally got home after football practice, he was exhausted and angry. He only made second string, but he would still have to go to practice every day and be a tackle dummy for all the big guys. But he couldn't even concentrate on

A desire to self-medicate can lead teens with anxiety disorders into risky behaviors, such as drinking alcohol or doing drugs.

practice because he was so worried about his homework. He hadn't realized high school would be so stressful. He had double the homework from last year, and his math teacher expected him to understand stuff he'd never seen before. There weren't enough hours in the day.

But he found a solution. His parents weren't home yet, so he unlocked the liquor cabinet and poured himself a little whiskey. His parents hid the key, but it hadn't been that hard to find. He had been having a drink after practice every day for the last couple of weeks. But this time he was so stressed he made it two. He knew he needed to start his homework, or he'd never get it all done. But he really wanted to relax first.

His parents always had a drink as soon as they got home from work. They needed it to relax, they said, and it seemed to work. Of course, they made a big deal about drinking being off limits for him because he was still a kid. "But why shouldn't it work for me, too?" he had thought the first time. And it definitely relaxed him. But after his second drink, he got very sleepy. He closed his eyes, and suddenly his mom and dad were standing over him, and his dad was shouting.

He tried to explain how stressed he was, and how he thought a drink would relax him

THE COST OF UNTREATED ANXIETY

"I think everyone can see that chronic drug abuse is a waste of potential. What's not as intuitive to many people is the terrible loss of potential in people with untreated psychiatric illness. When these kids don't get treatment they not only drink and do drugs more than other kids, they drop out of school, they hurt themselves, they have trouble holding a job and being good parents, [and] they have more physical symptoms and complaints as adults. The cost to the individual, and the rest of us, is very high."[1]

—*Harold S. Koplewicz, MD,*
President,
Child Mind Institute

the way it did for them. His argument didn't work. He was grounded. But at least his mom seemed to listen when he talked about feeling stressed. Maybe when she was less angry, they would be able to talk and work out another way to deal with his anxiety.

UNTREATED ANXIETY

Sometimes, untreated anxiety disorders lead to more severe problems. To feel better, some anxious teens try to self-medicate and become addicted to alcohol or drugs. Ethan, for example, knew his parents didn't want him to drink. Perhaps they had even discussed with him the dangers of teenage drinking. But his anxiety overcame his common sense. Others teens become depressed; some even consider or attempt suicide. Suicide is the third leading cause of death among young people aged 15 to 24.[2] Other teens, particularly girls, resort to self-injury or develop eating disorders.

DRUG AND ALCOHOL ABUSE

The more anxious or depressed you are, the greater your risk for addiction to tobacco, alcohol, and other drugs. Approximately 20 percent of Americans with mood disorders such as anxiety or depression also have an alcohol or substance abuse problem.[3] Unfortunately, alcohol and drugs often make anxiety symptoms worse.

The developing teenage brain is particularly sensitive to alcohol and drugs. Teens tend to engage in binge drinking—drinking large quantities of alcohol at one time. This causes dangerous problems, including alcohol poisoning and blackouts, as well as a greatly increased risk of developing alcoholism. One study showed excessive marijuana use in teens before age 18 caused a decreased IQ. Heavy marijuana users lost eight IQ points by age 38.[4] Mild users and those who began use after adolescence did not show the same declines.

EATING DISORDERS

An eating disorder involves a severe disturbance and lack of control of eating patterns. The person is excessively concerned about body weight or shape. He or she might eat far too much or far too little. Distorted eating habits may lead to life-threatening conditions. Approximately two-thirds of people with eating disorders also have anxiety disorders or OCD. The anxiety disorder usually develops first, often in childhood. Eating disorders include anorexia nervosa, bulimia nervosa, and "eating disorders not otherwise specified" (EDNOS), which

SYMPTOMS OF EATING DISORDERS

Anorexia Nervosa	Bulimia Nervosa
Extreme thinness (emaciation)	Alternate binging and purging
Extremely restricted eating and pursuit of thinness	Chronically sore, inflamed throat
Lack of menstruation; infertility	Swollen salivary glands
Thinning of bones	Worn tooth enamel; tooth decay
Brittle hair and nails	Acid reflux disorder
Dry, yellowish skin	Intestinal distress and irritation
Anemia; muscle wasting and weakness	Severe dehydration from purging
Low blood pressure; slow breathing and pulse	Electrolyte imbalance, possibly leading to heart attacks
Drop in body temperature	
Lethargy and tiredness	
Brain and heart damage; organ failure	

includes binge-eating disorder. Most sufferers are women. But approximately 5 to 15 percent of people with anorexia and bulimia and 35 percent with binge-eating disorder are men.[5]

People with anorexia nervosa see themselves as overweight even when they are dangerously thin. Many have symptoms of OCD and become obsessed with losing weight. They skip meals, pick at their food, limit themselves to a few types of food, weigh food portions, or cut each portion into tiny pieces. They may weigh themselves repeatedly or exercise obsessively to avoid weight gain. This results in dangerous malnourishment and medical problems, and in some cases even death.

People with bulimia eat unusually large amounts of food at once and then purge themselves by vomiting or overusing laxatives or diuretics, which stimulate food loss through diarrhea or increased urination. They might follow each eating binge with fasting or bouts of excessive exercise. Even though their weight appears normal, they fear gaining weight. They also suffer from digestive problems and dehydration.

Binge-eating disorder involves frequent bouts of overeating without purging as bulimics do. Binge eaters are often obese but keep repeating the cycle due to guilt and shame. Besides anxiety and depression, binge eaters often have medical conditions related to obesity, including heart disease and high blood pressure.

SELF-INJURIOUS BEHAVIOR

Self-injury is "any repetitive, socially unacceptable behavior resulting in mild to moderate physical injury, without suicidal intention."[6] Most teens who self-injure are girls from middle- or upper-class backgrounds with very low self-esteem. Usually they cut themselves with razors or other sharp objects, but they may also pick at skin or wounds or burn or hit themselves.

Some teens are so anxious or depressed that they feel numb, and they cut themselves to feel sensations. Others use the physical pain of cutting to take their minds off the pain of negative emotions. Some are trying to communicate their pain, but some are secretive and hide the self-injury from others. A person who self-injures does not intend to commit suicide, but self-injury is addictive and is an extremely poor coping tool. If not treated, self-injuring teens may eventually escalate from self-injury to suicide.

DEPRESSION AND SUICIDE

Depression occurs with all types of anxiety disorders. Depressed teenagers often have low self-esteem, but they do not always appear sad. Sometimes, they express depression as irritability, anger, aggression, or rage. They might have unexplained aches and pains, be extremely sensitive to criticism, or withdraw from some (but not necessarily all) of their friends. Depression can lead to problems at school, running away, reckless behavior, drug or alcohol abuse, or even violence.

The combination of anxiety and depression often leads to suicidal thoughts and actions. People with social anxiety disorder and OCD have a higher risk for suicide than the general public. As many as 18 percent of people diagnosed with panic disorder attempt suicide, and 38.5 percent have suicidal thoughts.[7] The risk is greater if the person is also depressed.

According to the Centers for Disease Control and Prevention (CDC), every year approximately 14 percent of teenagers consider suicide, 11 percent have a suicide plan, and 6 percent attempt suicide.[8] Some suicide attempts are cries for help, but an increasing

MOOD DISORDERS IN GIRLS

Before puberty, boys and girls have approximately the same incidence of anxiety and depression, 3 to 5 percent. But during adolescence, girls are twice as likely as boys to be diagnosed with mood disorders. Their prevalence is as high as for adults, 14 to 20 percent.[9] Because girls' brains mature faster than boys' brains, they are more able to process emotional stimuli, making them more sensitive and more vulnerable to mood disorders.

If a friend is talking about death or suicide, it is important to tell a trusted adult.

number are successful. Warning signs that a teen is suicidal include talking about committing suicide (even jokingly), writing about or romanticizing death, acting recklessly, giving away possessions, or saying good-bye to friends and family. These behaviors must always be taken seriously.

When anxiety disorders coexist with each other or with other disorders, especially depression, they can lead to severe consequences. Symptoms often overlap, and it is difficult to determine when an occasional behavior becomes a disorder. But anxiety disorders are very treatable. Early treatment can prevent anxiety disorders from progressing to more serious conditions.

ASK YOURSELF THIS

- *Do you think you have symptoms of more than one anxiety disorder, or are you depressed? What makes you think this?*

- *Have you ever tried cigarettes, alcohol, or other drugs to decrease your anxiety? Is this a useful coping tool? Why or why not?*

- *Do you have an eating disorder? If so, do you think it is related to an anxiety disorder?*

- *Have you ever hurt yourself in an attempt to decrease anxiety or emotional pain? If so, do you consider this a useful coping tool? What other ways might you deal with anxiety?*

- *Have you ever had suicidal thoughts? Have you ever acted on these thoughts? Have you discussed them with an adult or a friend?*

HOW IS ANXIETY TREATED?

Javier had an eating disorder. He didn't feel good about his behavior, but he couldn't control it. He had been skipping meals, and when he did eat, he was very careful not to eat more than three bites of anything. He hoped he wouldn't gain weight if he cut the bites very

Eating a healthful diet can be one step in helping you stay calm and relaxed.

small. His therapist was helping him learn a new technique to try at home.

The technique was the "stepladder" approach. The therapist wanted Javier to make very small changes every day and work his way up the "ladder" until his eating habits returned to normal. Javier was beginning the first step: at every meal that day he had to eat four bites of each food instead of three. That sounded like a lot of food, and Javier wasn't sure he could do it.

At breakfast, his mother gave him a small plate—half of what everyone else had—but it looked like a mountain of food to him. His little sister kept track of his bites. She counted until he ate four small bites of scrambled eggs, and she clapped delightedly. She looked so happy, he decided he could do it. He ate four tiny pieces of toast, washing them down with small sips of orange juice.

Later, during lunch at school, he saw his mother had cut his food into bites for him. She included eight bites of his favorite meatloaf. He appreciated the thought—that wasn't going to happen!—but he did manage four bites. That evening, at dinner with his family, taking four bites seemed a bit easier. He promised himself he would try four bites again the next day, and the day after that, he might even manage five.

GETTING HELP

Often teens find it difficult to ask for help, even if they are suffering a lot with anxiety. They might think, "I can live with it." They might be too embarrassed or think they would be bothering people. Some might even think their problems are so bad they can't be helped.

But perhaps you have decided things are not hopeless. You are willing to take charge and overcome your anxiety by seeking treatment. You have discussed your fears with your parents or other caring adults, and they are onboard. They want you to be happy and anxiety-free, and you are working together to find out what is needed to make a diagnosis, what treatments are available, and which treatment would be best for you. Where do you start?

DIAGNOSING ANXIETY DISORDERS

First, see your family doctor to make sure you don't have an underlying illness. Next, with the help of your doctor and perhaps your school counselor, you and your parents or guardians will choose a therapist who is trained to diagnose and help teens with mental health problems. You should feel comfortable with the therapist.

Your diagnosis will depend on several sets of information. The therapist will conduct a diagnostic interview. She will ask you a series of questions to determine the type and severity of your symptoms and how long you have had them. Then, she will compare your symptoms with a list of criteria in the *DSM-5*. She might also ask you to complete a written questionnaire.

The therapist will observe your responses during the interview. But since she will only see you for a short time, she will also ask other people for information. She will ask your parents to describe your current problems and your relationships. She will also ask about your medical history, previous mental health diagnoses and treatments, and family history of mental health problems. With your parents'

HOW YOUR SCHOOL CAN HELP

For many teens, anxiety does not affect school performance, but if it does or if you are uncomfortable in school, explaining the situation to a teacher or school counselor can help. If you feel comfortable discussing your anxiety on your own, go for it. But you should also consider asking a parent or guardian to meet with you and the teacher or counselor. Discuss your symptoms and needs, provide background information about your disorder, and ask for their help. Most school personnel are caring and will be glad to help. Once they are informed about your needs, you can bring up minor issues later and fix them before they become serious.

A therapist will diagnose you and suggest a course of treatment, if necessary.

permission, she may also talk to your family doctor, school counselor, or teachers. Using all of this information, she will determine which, if any, of the defined anxiety disorders you have.

Getting a diagnosis may be stressful, especially since you are already anxious and perhaps also shy and private. But remember that everyone involved wants to help you. They are not trying to invade your privacy; they are seeking information that will help them guide you in learning to cope with your anxiety.

COGNITIVE BEHAVIORAL THERAPY

The most common treatment for anxiety is cognitive behavioral therapy (CBT). Sometimes CBT is combined with medication. Treatment is designed to help teens identify the components of their anxiety (physical, cognitive, and behavioral), learn coping skills, and apply the skills so they can learn to face anxiety-producing situations. Some treatment programs also teach assertiveness, social skills, and problem solving.

A key skill in CBT is realistic thinking— learning to replace negative thinking patterns with more realistic ones. Anxious people often assume the worst is going to happen. Do you think, "I can't give a speech; I'll make a fool of myself"? This is unrealistic thinking. Or, do you think that if something even a little bad happens, it will be a catastrophe? When your parents are late coming home from a party, do you automatically assume, "They've been killed in an accident"? This is also very unlikely. Horrible things do happen, of course, but they are rare. As you practice this skill in CBT, your thought patterns will become more realistic, such as, "I'll be nervous, but I can do this," or "My parents probably just lost track of time."

CBT patients also learn breathing and relaxation techniques. Slow, regular breathing helps control the hyperventilation associated with anxiety and panic. Relaxation training involves teaching methods to relax your muscle groups one by one, which lowers anxiety levels. Finally, CBT patients are gradually exposed to factors associated with anxiety. In situational exposure, they receive training in coping strategies and then are repeatedly exposed to anxiety-provoking situations. The patients progress from the least to the most frightening situation. In interoceptive exposure, patients are gradually exposed to physical sensations felt during panic, such as dizziness, heart pounding, or hyperventilation. This helps them become more comfortable with the physical symptoms of anxiety.

CBT usually lasts approximately 12 weeks but has lifelong benefits. The process involves "homework" to practice the techniques learned in

CREATING A STEPLADDER

Situational exposure is a "stepladder" approach. You set up a list of situations, starting with the least frightening and progressing to those that frighten you most. Practice each "step" repeatedly until your fear disappears before moving up to the next step. As you progress up the stepladder, you become less fearful and more confident. A person who fears spiders might begin by looking at a picture of a spider. When they can do that without anxiety, they progress to looking at a spider in a sealed jar, and so on, until they can touch or hold a spider without fear.

Your CBT treatment is designed to help you cope with challenging and stressful situations.

therapy in real life. Often parents or guardians are also involved.

Medications can be used alone but are most often used with CBT. Medications used to treat anxiety regulate signals in the brain. Use can be either short term or long term, depending on the patient's symptoms and how well he or she responds to the medication. One large study showed a combination of therapy and medication worked better for children and teens aged seven to 17 than either treatment alone.[1] With severe anxiety symptoms, medication is sometimes used to suppress anxiety enough for behavioral therapy to work.

The main thing to remember is that anxiety can be treated. For mild to moderate anxiety, you will probably use a form of CBT to learn how to manage your thoughts and behaviors. If your anxiety is severe or if you have more than one condition, your therapist might also prescribe medication. Your treatment will be tailored specifically to your needs. These treatments do not cure everyone, but approximately 55 to 60 percent of children and teens recover from an anxiety diagnosis following CBT or related treatments.[2] CBT may not completely rid you of your anxiety symptoms, but it helps

TYPES OF ANXIETY MEDICATIONS

The most commonly used medications are selective serotonin reuptake inhibitors (SSRIs), which are effective against both anxiety and depression. SSRIs are preferred because they are mild and usually have few side effects. Some brand-name SSRIs include Zoloft and Prozac. Although SSRIs usually have few side effects, the US Food and Drug Administration has issued a warning that a small percentage of children and adolescents respond to these drugs with suicidal thoughts or actions. If you are taking medication, it is vital to follow your therapist's advice carefully and tell your parents or guardians and therapist immediately if you have any side effects, including suicidal thoughts.

Serotonin–norepinephrine reuptake inhibitors (SNRIs) are prescribed for panic attacks. SNRIs include Cymbalta and Effexor. Benzodiazepines, a class of mild sedatives, are also effective against panic attacks. These drugs include Xanax and Valium. However, they can be habit forming in high doses or if taken for long time periods, and they have dangerous interactions with alcohol.

many people. It is important to be patient. You are learning to change thought patterns and developing new habits. That takes time! So, there is hope—and the sooner you begin treatment, the sooner you will feel better.

ASK YOURSELF THIS

- *Are you willing to consider seeking help to learn to manage your anxiety? Have you discussed your concerns with your parents, guardians, or another trusted adult?*

- *Do you think you can clearly communicate to a therapist the most important symptoms of your anxiety and how anxiety is affecting your life? What would you say?*

- *How do you think the CBT process would affect your anxiety?*

- *What negative thought patterns, if any, might you need to change to relieve your anxiety?*

- *Would you feel comfortable taking medications for anxiety if your therapist recommended them? Why or why not?*

6

A LESS STRESSFUL LIFE

sabel was recently diagnosed with GAD and
social anxiety disorder. The night before her
first appointment with her new therapist, she
was worried about what to say. She talked to
her mother about her fears. At least she could

joke about it. "Of course, I'm worried—that's the whole point of going. I worry about everything!"

Her mother laughed too, but said, "I think we can help with your anxiety about tomorrow. Let's plan what you want to say to Dr. Gregory. You can make a list of topics and take it with you."

They worked together to decide on topics. First, they decided that Isabel needed to list all the things she was afraid of. "That's a long list," Isabel said wryly. "That's okay," her mom said. "Maybe it will be shorter after your sessions." Then, they listed her symptoms—including sweating, flushing, and rapid heartbeat when she faced frightening situations.

Finally, they tried to think about how her fears affected her life. Isabel felt she was missing a lot of fun things her friends were doing. For example, because she was afraid of the water, she wouldn't go to the pool or the beach. Her schoolwork was suffering too. She was deathly afraid of performing in public, which meant low grades on class presentations.

Isabel was embarrassed at the thought of revealing so much about herself, but her mother reminded her it was the therapist's job to listen. Isabel decided she must be honest and thorough to get the help she needed. As she put

Staying active is part of a healthy, low-stress lifestyle.

her completed list in her purse, she felt more relaxed and ready for her appointment.

LIFESTYLE CHANGES FOR MANAGING STRESS

Stress is part of every teen's life. Most stresses center on family, friends, and school. As an anxious teen, you can learn ways to manage stress and anxiety. Some of these techniques are things you should be doing anyway, like getting enough sleep, eating a healthful diet, and getting plenty of exercise. All of these will calm you and keep you healthy. In addition, you can learn specific techniques for managing your stress.

EATING A HEALTHFUL DIET

What you put into your body controls how it functions. As a teenager, you are still growing and developing, so you need energy and the right kinds of nutrients. Eating healthfully might be hard to do. It's easy to skip meals, grab a snack from a vending machine, choose a sugary soda over a glass of water, or eat a doughnut instead of an apple. But failing to eat a healthful diet may compromise your physical, mental, and emotional health.

Healthful eating requires balance and moderation. Eat a balanced diet including food from all food groups every day, and eat moderate portions of everything. The most recent recommendations from the US federal government are contained in the 2010 Dietary Guidelines for Americans (DGA). Your plate

GETTING ENOUGH EXERCISE

Aerobic exercise—the kind that gets your heart rate up—also gets your blood flowing, strengthens your muscles, and combats high blood pressure. It helps you think more clearly and calms your mind. But as a teenager, you often exercise less. Although some of your peers get exercise through competitive sports, perhaps you don't want to compete that way. If your activity levels have decreased, it's time to get back into the exercise groove. Make it a habit to be active every day. The type of exercise doesn't matter. It might be as simple as walking, running, or climbing stairs. You might skateboard or go hiking, biking, swimming, or dancing. It might be a solo activity, a team activity, or something you do with a friend. Just move!

should consist of approximately one-half fruits and vegetables (preferably fresh), one-fourth proteins (meat, beans, and nuts), and one-fourth grains and starches (whole-grain bread, other whole grains, and potatoes). The calcium in dairy products is also essential for teens.

FOODS AND DRINKS THAT WORSEN ANXIETY

Some foods and drinks may trigger or increase anxiety. These include caffeine, which is found in cola, coffee, tea, and chocolate, as well as alcohol and nicotine.

GETTING ENOUGH SLEEP

According to experts, teens need nine or more hours of sleep per night. But on school nights, the average for kids ages 11 to 17 is only 7.5 hours.[1] Even sleeping late on weekends doesn't make up for the seven or more hours of sleep lost during the week.

Lack of sleep begins a vicious cycle. It's hard to wake up, and you feel groggy and tired. You load up on caffeine to stay awake in class. You go to practices and meetings, and you stay up late doing homework. Your anxiety level skyrockets, and your grades and performance in other activities suffer. You're less alert, so if you drive, you're more likely to have an accident.

If you suspect you're not getting enough sleep, keep a journal of your sleep habits. How much sleep do you get? When do you go to bed and get up? What disturbs your sleep? If you decide you are not getting enough sleep, set a regular sleep schedule and stick to it. Do only relaxing things before bedtime. You might be surprised how much your anxiety improves!

MANAGING STRESS

To deal with daily stress and anxiety, you must figure out what factors and situations are causing your anxiety. First, make sure you can identify the signs of stress in your body. Are you jittery and irritable? Is it difficult to concentrate? Are your muscles tight? Do you frequently feel tearful or emotional? Now, think of factors that cause you to feel these symptoms. Consider your family life, school, friends, and other places and situations. Make a list, and be as specific as you can.

GOOD SLEEP HABITS

- Set a consistent bedtime and wake-up time.
- Don't drink caffeinated beverages after lunch.
- Don't eat or exercise for one to two hours before bedtime.
- Turn off electronics one to two hours before bedtime; read or listen to music instead.
- Keep your bedroom for sleeping, not homework or television, and make it relaxing.
- Use a non-illuminating clock.
- If you can't sleep, get up and read or do another quiet activity. Let sleep come naturally.

Often, your stressors represent problems you need to solve or changes you need to make. Rather than letting anxiety overtake you, you can take charge and learn to solve these problems. Do this in a step-by-step way. When you begin to feel symptoms of anxiety, immediately identify the stressor. Then, define the problem it is causing you. Make a list of potential solutions. Identify the pros and cons of each solution and then pick the one that seems best. Apply that solution. Do you feel less anxious? If so, congratulations! You are learning to control your anxiety.

MANAGING RELATIONSHIPS

When you are anxious, you may feel alone or feel that no one understands you. Learning to communicate effectively with family members and friends can go a long way toward controlling your anxiety. One way to improve communication is to practice assertiveness. Some people are too passive, not expressing their opinions or wishes, or too aggressive, being pushy and always putting their own wishes ahead of others'. Being assertive is a middle ground. You express your own opinions and feelings politely, while also considering the opinions and feelings of others. This opens the possibility of discussing the situation and getting at least some of what you want or need.

Sometimes having anxiety disorders makes you feel isolated. It is important to practice effective communication with others.

Many people with anxiety disorders have difficulty interacting with other people. This is not the case for all disorders, but often teens with social phobia or GAD are very uncomfortable even talking to other people. Sometimes these teens know how to respond in a social situation, but they are so anxious they are unable to do it. In other cases, they may not know what to do or have had very little practice interacting socially, so they are unsure and unwilling to take the risk. In either case, improving your social skills can go a long way toward decreasing anxiety.

Learning social skills takes practice and experience. Practice your skills with parents and friends, starting with the simplest body language skills and gradually adding higher-level skills. Observe how other people perform these skills—you might watch adults, classmates, or even people on television. Look for opportunities to use the skills in your everyday life. You will not become a smooth and accomplished conversationalist overnight, and you will not always do a good job of standing up for yourself. But that's okay! No one is perfect, and people will not stop being friendly just because you stumble a little. In any case, good social skills

The five types of social skills build on one another. You must learn earlier skills before you can develop later ones.	
Social Skill	Examples
Body language	Eye contact, appropriate posture, and facial expressions
Voice quality	Tone, pitch, volume, rate, and clarity of speech
Conversation	Greetings and introductions, starting and carrying out conversations, choosing topics, being polite
Friendship	Offering help, inviting people to join activities or visit, asking to join activities, expressing affection, giving compliments, being caring, showing empathy
Assertiveness	Standing up for oneself, asking for help or expressing need, saying no, dealing with teasing and bullying

are an important tool to add to your present and future anxiety-busting arsenal.

ASK YOURSELF THIS

- *Can you think of ways your diet could be improved? Do you think changing your diet would help your anxiety?*

- *Do you get enough sleep? If not, why not? What changes could you make to improve your sleep habits?*

- *Do you get enough exercise? What changes could you make to be more active?*

- *What factors in your life cause the most stress? How can you make these factors less stressful?*

- *Are there people in your life with whom you would like to have a better relationship? What can you do to accomplish this?*

7

ALTERNATIVE TREATMENTS FOR ANXIETY

It had been a month since the shooting at her school, and Ladonna was still having nightmares. She woke up nearly every night drenched with sweat, remembering her friends lying in the parking lot soaked in blood. Fortunately, no one died, but she hadn't known

Slow breathing and emptying your mind of thoughts are yoga and meditation techniques that might help your anxiety.

that at the time. As she lay in bed, she closed her eyes and repeated the affirmations the school counselor suggested:

I am safe and secure.

I am grateful to be alive.

I am letting go of the past and living in the present moment.

After she repeated each statement several times, she felt calmer. She got up and got ready for school. She was still nervous about going, but it was getting a little easier every day. The group counseling sessions were really helping.

Ladonna's mother drove her to school. Before leaving the car, Ladonna sat quietly and breathed deeply while pressing the acupressure points the counselor taught them. First, she did the Sea of Tranquility, pressing her middle fingers into her breastbone at heart level. Then, she did Wind Mansion, pressing the fingers into the hollow at the base of her skull. Finally, she did Third Eye, pressing the hollow just above her nose with both forefingers.

Ladonna felt ready to tackle another school day. It was amazing that pressing these points relieved her anxiety, but it really worked for her. She felt grateful to know techniques to relieve her anxiety, and she promised herself to use them regularly.

COMBINING ALTERNATIVE TREATMENTS WITH MEDICAL TREATMENT

In a psychotherapy program such as CBT, you will learn anxiety-reducing techniques that you must practice in daily life as you encounter anxiety-producing situations. Your therapist might also suggest one or more alternative remedies. This might include relaxation techniques such as visualization, meditation, and yoga. Several herbal remedies are used to treat anxiety, but their risks and benefits have not been thoroughly studied. Two other alternative techniques, biofeedback and the acupressure Ladonna used, lead to physical changes that also help you relax.

Alternative or complementary therapies for anxiety treatment appeal to people because they are holistic, or consider a person's body, mind, and spirit. Other people choose alternative approaches because they fear and mistrust conventional treatments, particularly medications. They may also avoid medical help because they fear the stigma of a mental disorder.

Alternative therapies such as yoga, meditation, or controlled breathing might be the only therapy you need if your anxiety is relatively minor. But often these therapies

Putting pressure on certain spots on the body can relieve stress.

are used together with conventional medical treatment. In all cases, it is important to use alternative therapies under the guidance of your therapist.

BREATHING AND MUSCLE RELAXATION

Relaxation therapy can take many forms, including controlled breathing, yoga, meditation, and visualization or imagery. Many of these have been used for millennia in India, China, and Tibet, but they have only recently been studied in Western medicine.

Controlled breathing will likely be one of the first techniques your therapist will teach you.

ABDOMINAL BREATHING HOW-TO

- Find a quiet, comfortable spot and close your eyes.
- Breathe in deeply through your nose and out through your mouth.
- Inhale slowly, thinking the word *calm*. Pause for a count of three.
- Exhale slowly, thinking the word *mind*. Pause for a count of three.
- Repeat these breaths for ten to 15 minutes.

It is easy to learn, can be practiced anywhere quiet, and will rapidly lower your anxiety levels. You breathe slowly and deeply, completely filling and emptying your lungs. After you calm your mind and relax your body by controlled breathing, you can begin using other anxiety-reducing tools.

Progressive muscle relaxation is also a simple technique that can be practiced almost anywhere. You alternately contract and then relax the muscles of each body region. Many athletes and musicians use both controlled breathing and progressive muscle relaxation to prepare themselves before a game or a concert.

YOGA, MEDITATION, AND VISUALIZATION

Hatha yoga, the type of yoga usually practiced in the United States, consists of physical poses combined with controlled breathing. It is followed by a short period of deep relaxation or meditation. People who practice yoga feel less stress and anxiety, and their heart rates, respiration rates, and blood pressure all decrease. Yoga practitioners also feel less pain and are more able to respond flexibly to stress.

PROGRESSIVE MUSCLE RELAXATION

Relax each muscle group in turn, tensing for 15 seconds and then relaxing for 15 seconds before moving to the next group. Do muscle groups in this order: face and head, neck and shoulders, hands and arms, abdomen, and legs and feet.

Similar to yoga, people have practiced meditation for thousands of years. In the past, it was used to help people understand the sacred aspects of life; today, it is also often used to calm the mind and achieve deep relaxation. To meditate properly, you must relax your breathing and focus your attention. Beginning practitioners often find meditation easier in a calm, quiet place. Advanced practitioners can often meditate in loud, anxiety-filled situations, at the times when they need stress relief the most. In transcendental meditation, you choose a mantra and repeat it silently to yourself, trying to achieve stillness and eliminate distracting thoughts. In mindfulness meditation, you try to be mindful, or very aware of the

A SIMPLE VISUALIZATION

- Choose a quiet location, lie comfortably on your back, and close your eyes.
- Imagine a calm place you would like to be, perhaps a warm, quiet beach or beside a flowing stream in a cool forest.
- Using all your senses, explore your calm place, imagining it in detail.
- Become aware of your muscles relaxing and notice your breathing and heart rate slowing.
- Notice that your mind is becoming calm and quiet as you focus your energy on exploring your calm place.
- Stay in your calm place as long as you need to.

present moment. You let thoughts and emotions flow through you, trying not to respond to them.

Visualization, or guided imagery, is a form of meditation in which you choose a mental image of something that relaxes you. You might choose a place such as a beautiful, warm beach or a peaceful forest. You use all your senses to visualize your image. What do you see and hear? What do you smell? What textures do you feel? Using this image, you relax yourself as completely as possible. You may do this by yourself or have a helper or teacher guide you. Some teens write out their image, record someone reading it, and play it back during each session.

BIOFEEDBACK AND ACUPRESSURE

Biofeedback helps you control your body's involuntary functions, such as heart rate and blood pressure, which in turn relaxes you. In a biofeedback session, a therapist attaches electrodes to your skin. While you practice a relaxation technique, such as deep breathing or meditation, the electrodes send information about your body functions to a monitor. The monitor responds to changes with a sound, flash of light, or image. The monitor teaches you to relax by showing you the changes in your body functions, so you know when you are succeeding. Over time, you learn to recognize body changes and no longer need the monitor. Through biofeedback, you can train yourself to relax and release your anxiety. Then later, for example, if you suffer a panic attack, you will be able to stop or diminish it by lowering your heart

ACUPRESSURE ROUTINE FOR ANXIETY AND PANIC ATTACKS

Several acupressure points are useful to counteract anxiety and panic attacks. Press these points for several minutes while breathing deeply. Three points are:

- **Sea of Tranquility:** center of breastbone; best point to use during a panic attack
- **Letting Go:** three finger-widths below collarbone, on upper, outer side of chest; use when you feel a panic attack coming on
- **Inner Gate:** three finger-widths above wrist; relieves anxiety and nausea

*An acupuncturist inserts small needles
at exact spots on the body.*

rate and breathing rate and reducing muscle
contractions.

   You might have heard of acupuncture,
a form of Chinese medicine in which very
thin needles are inserted into the body at
specific points to control the body's flow of
energy. Acupressure uses the same points
but stimulates them using the pressure of
hands and fingertips instead of needles. It has
a long history of relieving stress and anxiety
by decreasing muscle tension, improving
blood circulation, and affecting other physical

functions. A major benefit of acupressure is that once you learn the acupressure points, you can use them on yourself.

HERBAL REMEDIES

Several herbal remedies are used to treat anxiety, but currently most of them are either not well tested or have serious side effects. Thus, you should never take an herbal remedy for anxiety without first talking to your doctor, especially if you are taking other medications. The most common botanicals thought to decrease anxiety are kava, valerian root, and passionflower. However, kava has been associated with serious liver damage and has been pulled off the market in some European

HERBAL REMEDIES: USES AND SIDE EFFECTS

Remedy	Function	Known Side Effects
Kava	To treat anxiety	Potential severe liver damage
Valerian	To treat sleeplessness and mild anxiety; research on anxiety limited	Headaches, drowsiness; do not take with sedatives or antihistamines
Passionflower	To treat anxiety	Drowsiness, dizziness, confusion, nausea; do not take with sedatives or during pregnancy

Many people find listening to music helps them relax.

countries. The US Food and Drug Administration
has issued warnings about its use. Two common
(and safe) vitamin supplements, B-vitamins
and omega-3 fatty acids, have been shown to
improve both anxiety and depression.

Alternative therapies, particularly relaxation
methods, can be valuable additions to your
anxiety treatment. You can use many of
them throughout your life to control anxiety.
You can also practice other natural methods

of relaxation, from listening to music to aromatherapy to self-hypnosis. The important thing is you learn to relax both your mind and your body.

ASK YOURSELF THIS

- *Which alternative treatments do you think would be most helpful to you?*

- *Which treatments can you learn and practice on your own, and which would require (or benefit from) the help of a friend? Which would need to be directed by your therapist?*

- *Are you willing and able to make an alternative treatment such as controlled breathing or yoga a part of your daily routine?*

- *How can you use alternative techniques to calm your mind and reduce the physical symptoms of anxiety?*

- *Would you be comfortable taking an herbal remedy as part of your anxiety treatment? Do your parents or guardians and therapist think this is a good idea?*

8

WHERE DO I TURN FOR HELP?

Kareem had been anxious for a long time, but he always tried to hide it. For example, he made excuses to avoid doing things that scared him. Finally, because he knew he was missing a lot, he discussed his problems with his parents and got help.

It might be hard to start the conversation, but telling your friends about your anxiety will likely help you feel better.

He began doing CBT. But he knew he needed to tell his best friends, Jake and Isaac, what was going on. He hoped they'd even be willing to help. As they walked home together after school, he tried to explain.

"Do you guys remember when you took that trip to the theme park, and I said I couldn't go because my parents had something planned?" Kareem began.

"Yeah, you missed a great trip," Jake said. "Those rides were awesome."

"Well, we didn't really have something planned. I lied. I didn't go because I was afraid." There, he'd said it.

His friends were staring at him. "Afraid of what?" Isaac asked.

"I know it sounds dumb," Kareem said, "but I have an anxiety disorder. Several, actually. There are things I'm deathly afraid of—like those rides. I don't want to be that way; I just can't control it. But I'm trying to overcome the fears, and I would really like your help."

"Well, sure," Isaac said. "We'll be glad to help." Jake nodded agreement. "You just have to tell us what we can do."

"But you know we're going to give you a hard time about this, don't you?" Isaac said, grinning at him. Kareem grinned back. "Yeah,

I know," he said. "I can take it, as long as you promise to keep it between us."

DEVELOPING A SUPPORT TEAM

As you work to overcome your anxiety disorder, you will do much of the work yourself—you will learn and practice relaxation exercises, gradually confront the situations that make you anxious, and in general learn to take control of your anxieties. But you will need help. No one should have to confront anxiety problems alone. There are many people in your life willing and eager to help you, from family and friends to medical professionals to members of online organizations.

A good team can support you emotionally and remind you to use your anxiety-reducing tools. But be careful when choosing your support team. Choose only a few adults and friends who are most likely to understand your situation.

In most cases, teens begin by talking with one or both parents or guardians. But if you don't think they would understand, look for another adult who will listen. This might be a school counselor, teacher, coach, family doctor, or leader in your church, synagogue, or mosque. Or try an older sibling or close friend. Be sure the person you choose respects you, takes your anxiety seriously, and is willing to keep your confidences private. Explain your anxieties as clearly as possible and ask if this person is willing to be your support person, who will always be there, even if only by e-mail, when you need help. If the first person you ask doesn't feel they can take on the responsibility, don't be discouraged. Simply look for someone else.

Besides an adult support person, confide in one or two close friends and ask for their support. They should be close and trusted people you can confide in. You should feel comfortable around them. You will likely find most people are very willing to help when they understand the situation.

Your therapist is an extremely important part of your support team. At first, you might feel anxious about telling your problems to a stranger. But this is the person who is most able

HOW DO I EXPLAIN MY ANXIETY TO OTHERS?

When you talk to someone about your anxiety, figure out what you want to say in advance. Set up a time and place where you can talk privately. Explain that you want to discuss your anxiety, but the information you are sharing is personal and must be kept private. Then, explain how you are feeling. List your symptoms and explain why they are a problem. Explain how you are dealing with your anxiety problem and ask for the person's help. Be precise about what you hope the person will do.

to help you. You can reassure yourself by asking questions at your first meeting. Is the therapist trained in working with anxiety disorders? Does he or she have experience working with adolescents? Ask these and any other questions that bother you so you can feel secure working with the therapist. If you feel this therapist is not a good fit, talk with your support person about finding someone else.

WHAT DO I SAY TO A THERAPIST?

At your first meeting, you should ask questions about the therapist's qualifications and experience. You should make sure he or she will keep your conversations private. If you are under 18, your parents can talk with your therapist, so you should discuss with everyone what information you want the therapist to share. In most states, parents must give consent for children under 18 to meet with a therapist. Also, you might ask how the process will work—for example, how the therapist will help you set goals, how many sessions will likely be needed, what techniques you will learn, and whether he or she is open to feedback from you. Finally, you should answer all questions honestly, so your work together will be helpful.

ONLINE SUPPORT

There is helpful information online, but it is important to choose online resources carefully. Your doctor or therapist might suggest useful Web sites. Sites associated with specific hospitals or professional organizations,

including the Mayo Clinic and the Anxiety
and Depression Association of America, have
trustworthy information. In addition, there are
blogs, forums, and support groups geared
especially toward people with anxiety disorders.
Some are specifically for teens. When you join
one of these groups, you can log in, tell your
story or ask a question, and receive advice
and support from people in the same situation.
Some sites have psychiatrists who will answer

HOW CAN I HELP MY FRIEND WITH ANXIETY?

If you have a friend suffering from an anxiety disorder,
you should first just be a friend. But you can also help in
several specific ways:

- Encourage your friend to talk to a therapist
  if she or he is not already doing so. Ask what
  you can do to help with their therapy.
- Learn as much as you can about the
  person's specific disorder.
- Give focused criticism of a specific behavior
  that rejects the behavior, not the person.
- Do not be too accommodating, giving in to
  constant requests for reassurance, for example.
  But, set limits that will gradually stop the
  behavior. Discuss this in advance, so the anxious
  person understands this is meant to help.
- If you are comfortable doing so, coach your
  anxious friend. Set goals for relieving anxiety, set
  a schedule, and work on meeting the goals.
- If you are coaching your friend, work with him or her to
  put the goals in writing. Make a contract that outlines
  the responsibilities of both people and sets a time limit.
- Don't allow yourself to become frustrated. This will
  increase your friend's anxiety and yours as well.

Some teens find online groups very supportive in helping them handle their anxiety.

questions and offer support. Others have blogs or articles by experts and ongoing discussions.

However, although online support can be very helpful, it is not a substitute for proper professional care. It should be used in combination with the treatment offered by your therapist or mental health practitioner.

WORKING AS A TEAM

Learning to cope with your anxieties includes developing new skills and new patterns of thinking. These include everything from breathing and relaxation exercises to visualization and acupressure. You can learn and practice these skills on your own, but a support team makes the process much easier. Your therapist can teach you skills, and your parents and friends can help you as you practice them. For example, if they notice you are using unrealistic thinking, they can point it out. If you are very anxious about a situation, they can remind you to practice your breathing exercises. But perhaps the best thing they can do is just be there, supporting and encouraging you, so you know you are not alone.

ASK YOURSELF THIS

- *Who are the people you would most like to have on your support team?*

- *What do you want your support team members to do for you?*

- *How can you explain your anxieties to the people on your support team so they will understand how you feel and be able to help you?*

- *What qualities do you want in a therapist? What do you want him or her to do for you?*

- *What will be your responsibilities as part of the team?*

9

CURE OR TREATMENT? THE FUTURE OF ANXIETY DISORDERS

One evening after dinner, Mahala asked her parents if they could talk. She had been working for the past year on her social anxiety disorder and felt she had made some progress. But she still had a long way to go, and she was worried about the future.

Discussing your future with your parents will help you be prepared for whatever life throws at you.

"Now that I'm a junior," she told them, "I need to figure out what I'm going to do about college. I really want to go, but I'm not sure I can handle being away from home."

"Well, I'm glad you're thinking about college," her mother said. "That shows how much progress you've made. Do you think you could have even considered leaving home this time last year?"

"No," Mahala admitted. "I hadn't thought of it that way. But I'm still not sure I can do it."

"Remember," her dad said. "You have more than a year to decide, and by that time you might be ready. In the meantime, doesn't it make sense to plan for it, just in case?"

"You can handle getting ready for college the same way you've handled your other fears," her mother added. "Do it one step at a time. Now that you're feeling more comfortable in high school, why not think about taking a course at the community college? It's close to home, but it will still give you a feel for college. You could even go there for the first year or two and transfer to a four-year college later."

"You're right," Mahala said. "I guess I do have some options. College might be possible after all!"

LOOKING TOWARD THE FUTURE

Even as you work on decreasing your anxiety now, you are probably also worrying about the future. Will you always be anxious? Can you live a normal life? Can your anxiety ever be cured?

It's normal to be concerned about the future, but it's also impossible to give a single answer to questions like these. Because anxiety disorders and people vary so much, answers will differ for each person. Also, there might be advances in treatment just around the corner.

CURE VS. REMISSION

In treating anxiety, researchers distinguish between remission and response. *Remission* is the absence or near-absence of symptoms after treatment for a predetermined time period, while *response* is a meaningful improvement in symptoms. Remission is harder to accomplish than response, so it is less likely to occur.

Psychiatrist Dr. Franklin Schneier states that, overall, approximately one-fourth of anxiety patients receiving treatment show "stable remission over long periods of time," which is equivalent to a cure. These patients may have symptoms of anxiety, but symptoms are minor enough that patients are no longer diagnosed as having an anxiety disorder. Most patients show "meaningful improvement" after a single course of treatment.[1] Dr. Schneier points out, however, that their anxiety may recur, especially under high levels of stress.

Thus, evidence suggests that, while most people will improve with treatment, many will probably need to work on anxiety issues throughout their lives. This is especially true if you have a shy, inhibited personality or other genetic factors that contribute to your anxiety. The goal is not really to "cure" your anxiety—anxiety is a part of life. Anxiety helps you do your best and deal with stressful situations. The goal should be to learn to control your anxiety so it helps, rather than hurts, you.

SUCCESS OF TREATMENTS

In a 2011 study involving 488 children and adolescents ages seven to 17, researchers compared several anxiety treatments. The youth tested had separation, social, and/or generalized anxiety disorder. They were treated for 12 weeks with one of four treatments: medication only, CBT only, a combination of medication and CBT, or a pill placebo. The highest rates of remission (46 to 68 percent) occurred with the combination treatment; lower but still significant rates of remission occurred when either CBT or medication were given alone. Response rates were much higher than remission rates for all groups. Because some symptoms remained after 12 weeks, researchers concluded that extended treatment would probably be helpful.[2]

POSSIBLE FUTURE TREATMENTS

One problem with today's treatment for anxiety disorders is that many people are unable to find an affordable therapist working nearby who is taking more patients. Recently, researchers have tested online therapy as a way to make treatment more accessible. Treatments involved a series of online lessons, homework assignments, and weekly contact with either a clinician, a psychiatrist or psychologist, or a technician. Technicians are trained to carry out the treatments but do not have clinical training in psychiatry or psychology. In a 2010 study of 150 people who underwent ten weeks of online treatment for GAD, people in both the clinician and technician groups showed significant improvement.[3] In another study, 49 youths ages seven to 13 were divided into three groups: computer-assisted CBT, individual face-to-face CBT, and a control group providing "computer-assisted education, support, and attention" (CESA) but not CBT. Seventy percent and 81 percent of children in the two CBT groups showed relief of anxiety symptoms, while only 19 percent of the CESA group showed improvement.[4] Both studies suggest computer-assisted therapy for anxiety has great potential.

There is also ongoing research to learn more about the causes of anxiety disorders.

Researchers hope that better understanding the causes will lead to new treatments. One area of interest is the development of biomarkers, or biological indicators, to help predict which patients are likely to respond well to specific anxiety medications. Another potential treatment involves the use of brain-derived chemicals as medications. A chemical called brain-derived neurotrophic factor (BDNF) is being studied for its ability to cause the extinction of a fear response.

LIVING YOUR LIFE

Some teens will respond well to anxiety treatment and think they are "cured." Then, they suffer a relapse and feel anxious all over again. If this happens to you, don't panic! Try to figure out why it is happening. Did you stop

BDNFs—BRAIN DRUGS THAT EXTINGUISH FEAR

Extinction is the process of removing or weakening a conditioned behavior. This happens gradually if the response is no longer reinforced or rewarded. In a study with mice, extinction occurred under the influence of BDNF. Mice were first taught to fear a tone associated with a mild shock. When given BDNF, they "forgot" the fear; that is, it became extinct. Researchers think the drug changes connections between neurons in part of the brain. They hope it will lead to new treatments for anxiety disorders.

using the tools you learned, such as relaxation and realistic thinking? Has there been a major change in your life, such as a move to a new school? Did you recently have a particularly stressful or traumatic experience? Are school pressures building up, or are you being bullied? Try to identify and neutralize the cause, if possible. But, whatever the reason, go back to the tools and practice routine you used during treatment. Because you already know the tools, you should see much faster results this time. The important thing is to recognize the signs of anxiety and begin using your coping tools as quickly as possible. Constant practice of these coping tools is vital. You will be able to use them throughout your life to take charge of your anxiety.

DEALING WITH BULLYING

If you become the target of a bully, it's important to take charge of the situation. This won't be easy and bullying will still be hurtful. But with time and practice, you can develop responses that will make a bully decide you're not worth the effort. For example:

- Try to turn teasing into a joke; develop clever comebacks but don't be nasty or rude.
- Don't react emotionally; say or do something unrelated to the bully's words.
- Stay near a sympathetic friend or adult, and keep asking the bully to "say it louder." Eventually, the bully will get in trouble.
- To develop these skills, ask a parent or trusted friend to brainstorm or practice with you. If the bullying gets physical, get help from an adult immediately!

Enjoy your life and find fun activities to try!

One of the greatest gifts you can give
yourself as you work on decreasing your anxiety
is to keep a positive attitude and accept yourself

ANXIETY AND PERSONALIZED MEDICINE

Personalized medicine is the choice of a specific treatment based on a person's genetic information or other biological markers. For example, a functional magnetic resonance imaging (fMRI) brain scan can be used to determine treatments for GAD. In tests, an fMRI was done before and after treatment with an anxiety drug. Approximately two-thirds of patients showed decreased anxiety, with corresponding changes in their fMRIs. The fMRI could predict whether the treatment would work.

as a person. Every anxiety-busting tool you learn gives you more control of your life. Don't take these steps lightly—reward yourself for the progress you make. Enjoy time with friends and family. Try a new activity. Regain your sense of fun. Above all, remember your anxiety disorder is a real medical condition. It is not your fault or something you are doing wrong—but it is something you can learn to take control of.

ASK YOURSELF THIS

- *Do you worry whether your anxiety will continue in the future?*

- *Do you plan to continue using the coping skills you have developed, even after your anxiety gets better? Why or why not?*

- *Do you think it is important for doctors and researchers to understand more about the causes of anxiety disorders? Why or why not?*

- *Which social skills, if any, do you think you need to work on? Do you have a plan for doing this?*

- *What are the most important things you have learned about controlling your anxiety disorder?*

JUST THE FACTS

Anxiety is a response of worry or dread related to a future event. Anxiety becomes an anxiety disorder when the worry is disproportionate to the situation, disrupts your life, causes you distress, and has a long duration (months instead of days or weeks).

Approximately one of every 20 teens has an anxiety disorder. Girls have anxiety at a higher rate than boys.

Physical symptoms of anxiety result from prolonged stress and include muscle tension, headaches, and stomach upset as well as those related to the fight-or-flight response, including increased heart rate, breathing rate, and blood pressure; sweating; and dizziness.

Psychological symptoms of anxiety include irrational and excessive worry, dread, irritability, restlessness, and trouble concentrating.

Behavioral symptoms of anxiety include avoidance of people, situations, or activities; insomnia; always being alert for danger; and always expecting the worst.

Causes or risk factors leading to anxiety include genetic predisposition, a shy or inhibited personality, imbalances in hormones or brain neurotransmitters, overprotective parents or caregivers, fearful role models, and stressful or traumatic environmental factors. Those with a predisposition to anxiety may develop a disorder only in the presence of severe stress or trauma.

Untreated anxiety disorders can lead to serious complications, including alcohol and drug abuse, self-injury, and eating disorders. Approximately half of teens suffering from anxiety disorders also suffer from depression. The combination may lead to suicidal thoughts and actions.

To diagnose an anxiety disorder, a teen's symptoms are compared with those in the *DSM* published by the American Psychiatric Association. There are several designated types of anxiety disorders; however, people often have symptoms of more than one.

The major treatment for anxiety disorders is a form of therapy known as cognitive behavioral therapy (CBT). In CBT, the teen learns tools for controlling anxiety such as controlled breathing and muscle relaxation. He or she also learns to confront anxiety-producing situations slowly and to replace negative thinking with realistic thinking.

In some cases, medication is given to treat anxiety disorders. Sometimes it is given alone, but usually it is combined with CBT. The most common type of medications are SSRIs, or selective serotonin uptake inhibitors. These are mild and have few side effects. They act on neurotransmitters in the brain.

Approximately one-fourth of those treated for anxiety undergo remission, the apparently complete absence of symptoms. Most people show a response to treatment, or a meaningful reduction of symptoms. The goal of treatment is to control symptoms and to teach techniques that can be used throughout life to control anxiety when it arises.

WHERE TO TURN

If You're Anxious and Don't Know Where to Start

If you have reached a place where your anxiety is overwhelming you and interfering with your life, it's time to look for help. You must first talk to an adult who can understand how you feel and be a support person. Usually this is a parent, but it can also be a school counselor, teacher, or religious leader. You must feel comfortable confiding in the person, and he or she must be willing to keep your information private. Explain your feelings, including physical and emotional symptoms and behaviors, and describe how they are affecting your life. Work with your support person to find a therapist or counselor who can help you learn to control your anxiety.

If You Feel Alone with Your Anxiety Disorder

Most teens don't like to talk about their anxiety disorder and may even go to great lengths to hide it. But you are not alone. Everyone feels anxious and stressed at times; your anxiety is just greater than most people's. Developing a small support group will immediately help you feel less alone. Even though it might be scary, confide in one or two close friends. Tell them what you're going through and ask for their help. The most important thing they can do is to be your friend. But they might also help you practice your anxiety-busting exercises or remind you when you're being too anxious or using negative thinking. You can also join an online support group where you can talk to other teens with anxiety disorders, share stories, and help each other. One group is:
http://www.dailystrength.org/c/Teen-Anxiety/forum.

Learning to Live with Anxiety

If you have a shy, inhibited personality type, you probably tend to react to new things by avoiding them. This means you will probably have to work on anxiety issues throughout your life. This is not a major problem. Remember that anxiety in small doses is a good thing! You don't want to get rid of your anxiety; you just want to control it so it helps instead of hurts you. To do this, remember the tools you have learned to control your present anxiety. These include tools you learn during CBT, as well as breathing and relaxation techniques, yoga, meditation, or acupressure. Don't stop using these techniques just because you feel better. Make them a part of your life. This will enable you to control your anxiety when you encounter stressful or traumatic situations in the future.

If You Have a Panic Attack

First, learn to recognize the symptoms of a panic attack as it is beginning. Symptoms vary, but you'll probably feel like you're having a heart attack or even going crazy. You'll feel dizzy and short of breath and have a rapid, irregular heartbeat. As soon as this begins, breathe deeply and slowly. Sit or lie down and close your eyes. Relax your muscles, one group at a time, starting with your feet and moving upward. Or, you can try a different tactic. Instead of lying down, exercise. Walk in a quiet place, such as a park, or do yoga and stretching exercises, such as bending forward and touching your toes to the ground and holding that pose for ten seconds.

If Your Friend Has an Anxiety Disorder

If your friend has a diagnosed anxiety disorder, the first and best thing you can do is be a good friend. Be available when needed, offer support and encouragement, do things together, and continue to hang out together as you always have. In addition, if you are willing, you can do some specific things to help. Learn as much as you can about the specific condition. Listen to your friend's explanation, but also do research yourself. The more you know, the more you can help. If your friend is working on a specific fear and asks for your help, become a coach. Set goals, make a schedule, and work together to reduce his or her anxiety. You will both feel a sense of accomplishment!

GLOSSARY

compulsion
A repetitive behavior or mental act a person feels compelled to do in response to a perceived danger or obsession.

hormone
A chemical produced by an endocrine gland that travels through the bloodstream and controls body processes, including mood and behavior.

inhibited
Held back from acting freely or spontaneously by psychological or social limits.

mantra
A syllable, word, or phrase repeated while meditating.

neurotransmitter
A substance that transmits nerve impulses from one neuron to another.

obsession
An inappropriate, disturbing thought or image that constantly intrudes into a person's mind, causing anxiety and distress.

placebo
A substance or pill without therapeutic effect, used as a control in an experiment.

predisposition
Being more susceptible, or more likely, to have a disease due to genetic or other factors.

self-injury
Repetitive, socially unacceptable behavior resulting in physical injury, but without suicidal intent; may include cutting, burning, hitting, or picking at skin or scabs.

ADDITIONAL RESOURCES

SELECTED BIBLIOGRAPHY

Foa, Edna B., and Linda Wasmer Andrews. *If Your Adolescent Has an Anxiety Disorder: An Essential Resource for Parents*. New York: Oxford UP, 2006. Print.

Rapee, Ronald M., et al. *Helping Your Anxious Child*, Second Edition. Oakland, CA: New Harbinger, 2008. Print.

Tompkins, Michael, and Katherine Martinez. *My Anxious Mind: A Teen's Guide to Managing Anxiety and Panic*. Washington, DC: Magination, 2010. Print.

FURTHER READINGS

Anxiety Disorders. Farmington Hills, MI: Greenhaven, 2010. Print.

Donnelly, Kate Collins. *Starving the Anxiety Gremlin: A Cognitive Behavioural Therapy Workbook on Anxiety Management for Young People*. London, UK: Jessica Kingsley, 2013. Print.

Schab, Lisa M. *The Anxiety Workbook for Teens*. Oakland, CA: New Harbinger, 2008. Print.

Swigget, Chelsea. *Rae: My True Story of Fear, Anxiety, and Social Phobia*. Deerfield Beach, FL: Health Communications, 2010. Print.

WEB SITES

To learn more about living with anxiety disorders, visit ABDO Publishing Company online at **www.abdopublishing.com**. Web sites about living with anxiety disorders are featured on our Book Links page. These links are routinely monitored and updated to provide the most current information available.

SOURCE NOTES

CHAPTER 1. WHAT IS AN ANXIETY DISORDER?

1. Michael A. Tompkins, PhD, and Katherine Martinez, PsyD. *My Anxious Mind*. Washington, DC: Magination, 2010. Print. 6–7.

CHAPTER 2. TYPES OF ANXIETY DISORDERS

1. "Generalized Anxiety." *Anxiety BC*. Anxiety BC, n.d. Web. 7 Aug. 2013.

2. William T. Hey, PhD, Donna L. Bailey, MSE, and Kristine Stouffer, PhD. "Understanding Adolescent Anxiety Disorders: What Teachers, Health Educators, and Practitioners Should Know and Do." *International Electronic Journal of Health Education* 4 (2001): 83. *http://www.bvsde. paho.org*. Web. 7 Aug. 2013.

3. Edna B. Foa and Linda Wasmer Andrews. *If Your Adolescent Has an Anxiety Disorder: An Essential Resource for Parents*. New York: Oxford UP, 2006. Print. 17–18.

CHAPTER 3. WHY AM I LIKE THIS?

1. Edna B. Foa and Linda Wasmer Andrews. *If Your Adolescent Has an Anxiety Disorder: An Essential Resource for Parents*. New York: Oxford UP, 2006. Print. 19.

2. William T. Hey, PhD, Donna L. Bailey, MSE, and Kristine Stouffer, PhD. "Understanding Adolescent Anxiety Disorders: What Teachers, Health Educators, and Practitioners Should Know and Do." *International Electronic Journal of Health Education* 4 (2001): 81. *http://www.bvsde. paho.org*. Web. 7 Aug. 2013.

3. "Children and Teens." *Anxiety and Depression Association of America*. ADAA, n.d. Web. 7 Aug. 2013.

4. Ibid.

5. Edna B. Foa and Linda Wasmer Andrews. *If Your Adolescent Has an Anxiety Disorder: An Essential Resource for Parents*. New York: Oxford UP, 2006. Print. 36.

6. Ronald M. Rapee, Carolyn A. Schniering, and Jennifer L. Hudson. "Anxiety Disorders During Childhood and Adolescence: Origins and Treatment." *Ann. Rev. Clin. Psychol.* 5 (2009): 313. Print.

7. E. Jane Costello, PhD, Helen L. Egger, MD, and Adrian Angold, MRCPsych. "The Developmental Epidemiology of Anxiety Disorders: Phenomenology, Prevalence, and Comorbidity." *Child Adolesc Psychiatric Clin N Am* 14 (2005): 643–644. Print.

CHAPTER 4. CONSEQUENCES OF ANXIETY DISORDERS

1. Harold S. Koplewicz. "Does Teenage Pot Use Affect IQ?" *Child Mind Institute*. Child Mind Institute, 18 Sept. 2012. Web. 7 Aug. 2013.

2. Ron J. Steingard, MD. "Mood Disorders and Teenage Girls." *Child Mind Institute*. Child Mind Institute, 22 Jan. 2013. Web. 7 Aug. 2013.

3. "Substance Abuse." *Anxiety and Depression Association of America*. ADAA, n.d. Web. 7 Aug. 2013.

4. Harold S. Koplewicz. "Does Teenage Pot Use Affect IQ?" *Child Mind Institute*. Child Mind Institute, 18 Sept. 2012. Web. 7 Aug. 2013.

5. "Eating Disorders." *Anxiety and Depression Association of America*. ADAA, n.d. Web. 7 Aug. 2013.

6. Harold S. Koplewicz. "YouTube and Cutting: A Dangerous Combination." *Child Mind Institute*. Child Mind Institute, 29 Apr. 2011. Web. 7 Aug. 2013.

SOURCE NOTES CONTINUED

7. "Panic Disorder In-Depth Report: Possible Complications." *New York Times Health Guide*. New York Times, n.d. Web. 7 Aug. 2013.

8. "Many Teens Considering Suicide Do Not Receive Specialized Mental Health Care." *National Institute of Mental Health*. National Institutes of Health, 12 Oct. 2012. Web. 7 Aug. 2013.

9. Ron J. Steingard, MD. "Mood Disorders and Teenage Girls." *Child Mind Institute*. Child Mind Institute, 22 Jan. 2013. Web. 7 Aug. 2013.

CHAPTER 5. HOW IS ANXIETY TREATED?

1. "Children and Teens: Treatment." *Anxiety and Depression Association of America*. ADAA, n.d. Web. 7 Aug. 2013.

2. Ronald M. Rapee, Carolyn A. Schniering, and Jennifer L. Hudson. "Anxiety Disorders During Childhood and Adolescence: Origins and Treatment." *Ann. Rev. Clin. Psychol.* 5 (2009): 323. Print.

CHAPTER 6. A LESS STRESSFUL LIFE

1. Michael A. Tompkins, PhD, and Katherine Martinez, PsyD. *My Anxious Mind*. Washington, DC: Magination, 2010. Print. 138.

CHAPTER 7. ALTERNATIVE TREATMENTS FOR ANXIETY

None.

CHAPTER 8. WHERE DO I TURN FOR HELP?

None.

CHAPTER 9. CURE OR TREATMENT?
THE FUTURE OF ANXIETY DISORDERS

1. Franklin Schneier, MD. "Can Anxiety Disorder Be Cured?" *Ask the Experts*. Columbia Psychiatry, Columbia University Medical Center, n.d. Web. 7 Aug. 2013.

2. Golda S. Ginsburg, et al. "Remission after Acute Treatment in Children and Adolescents With Anxiety Disorders: Findings from the CAMS." *J Consult Clin Psychol*. 79.6 (Dec. 2011). PMC. Web. 7 Aug. 2013.

3. E. Robinson, et al. "Internet Treatment for Generalized Anxiety Disorder: A Randomized Controlled Trial Comparing Clinician vs. Technician Assistance." *PLoS ONE* 5.6 (2010): e10942. Web. 7 Aug. 2013.

4. Muniya S. Khanna and Philip C. Kendall. "Computer Assisted Cognitive Behavioral Therapy for Child Anxiety: Results of a Randomized Clinical Trial." *Journal of Consulting and Clinical Psychology* 78.5 (Oct. 2010). *PubMed*. Web. 7 Aug. 2013.

INDEX

ABOUT THE AUTHOR

Carol Hand has a PhD in zoology. She has taught college biology, written biology assessments and high school science curricula, and authored more than a dozen young-adult science books. She has had firsthand experience with teen anxiety disorders. Currently she works as a freelance writer of science books and online courses.